To my mom and dad, with love
—E.M.

Copyright © 2022 by Edward Miller

All rights reserved. Published in the United States by Random House Children's Books,
a division of Penguin Random House LLC, New York.

Random House and the colophon and Beginner Books and colophon are registered trademarks
of Penguin Random House LLC. The Cat in the Hat logo ® and © Dr. Seuss Enterprises, L.P.
1957, renewed 1986. All rights reserved.

Visit us on the Web!
rhcbooks.com

Educators and librarians, for a variety of teaching tools, visit us at RHTeachersLibrarians.com

Library of Congress Cataloging-in-Publication Data is available upon request.
ISBN 978-0-593-37725-3 (trade) — ISBN 978-0-593-37726-0 (lib. bdg.) —
ISBN 978-0-593-37727-7 (ebook)

MANUFACTURED IN THE UNITES STATES OF AMERICA
10 9 8 7 6 5 4 3 2
First Edition

BUSY STREET

Beep! Beep!

PARK

by Edward Miller

BEGINNER BOOKS®
A Division of Random House

Mommy's in the front seat,
out for a ride.
Bonnie's in the back seat,
eyes open wide.

On the street
in a busy town,
cars and trucks
go zipping round.

Left turns, right turns,
see them go—
some move fast
and some move slow.

A garbage truck,
hungry for trash,
chews and chomps
it into mash.

A sweeper gives
the street a bath.
Its big brush helps
to clean the path.

A tractor trailer
delivers goods
to supermarkets
in neighborhoods.

SCHOOL BUS

SCHOOL

SCHOOL CROSSING

A yellow bus
takes kids to school.
Some students walk,
and some carpool.

A paver works
on street repair,
filling holes
found here and there.

A road roller
smooths out the lumps
so drivers don't
ride over bumps.

A mail truck brings
letters and cards
to mailboxes
in people's yards.

A moving truck
has lots of space.
It carries things
from place to place.

Ring! Ring! Ring!

FIREHOUSE

Fire engines,
big and red,
race to clouds
of smoke ahead.

Big Red

Firefighters
are on the way.
They'll stop the fire
and save the day!

CAR DEALER

Big Savings

Great Deals

BIG BLUE

Low PRICE

Cars on a carrier,

double-stacked—

bumper-to-bumper

the cars are packed.

There's a red car, a green car—
that one is blue!
There's an orange car
and a purple one, too.

A bus is waiting
at the square.
Riders line up
to pay their fare.

A front-end loader
shows off its might
by moving rocks
at the construction site.

A concrete mixer
spins round and round,
then pours the concrete
onto the ground.

A crane truck's neck
can reach the sky.
It lifts materials
way up high.

A big dump truck
filled to the top
can tip its bed
to make a drop.

Honk!

Stopped at the light.
Why the delay?
The light is green. . . .
What's in the way?

PLAYGROUNd

HOP-123

A siren wails
and lights are flashing.
Cars move away
from the police car dashing.

An ambulance rushes
those who are ill
to the town's hospital
right up the hill.

The train is approaching—
down comes the gate.
The caboose passes slowly.
The cars have to wait.

An ice cream truck
sells a tasty treat.
Kids hear its song
from down the street.

A pizza van
delivers pies
with lots of toppings,
in any size.

A tow truck arrives
when a car needs a tug,
when it's out of gas
or it needs a plug.

A camper van
heads to the park
to set up camp
before it's dark.

Left turns and right turns,
driving around town.
It's getting late—
time to slow down.

LEFT
TURN

SLOW

All sorts of vehicles
out for a spin.
Oh, what fun
this ride has been!

Mommy's in the front seat,
she honks *beep, beep.* . . .
Bonnie's in the back seat,
fast asleep.

Beep!
Beep!

DOWN
TOWN →